Ordinary People can do extrordinary things!

Wolf's New Shoes

Rebecca Ballew Dockum
Author/Illustrator

Tim Traylor
Colorist

Alysha Coy Desharnais
Cover/Layout

ISBN 979-8-9881331-1-7

Cover/Layout: Alysha Coy Desharnias

Colorist :Tim Traylor

Author/Illustrator: Rebecca Ballew Dockum

Little Branch

PUBLISHING

$14.99
ISBN 979-8-9881331-1-7
51499>
9 798988 133117

Wolf the dog lives in Arizona.

Wolf's favorite person is Paisley.

They do everything together.

Paisley takes walks with Wolf.

But not today….

Mother had told them, “No walk today.
It’s too hot for Wolf’s paws.
He needs shoes.”

“Shoes?” Paisley asked.

“Shoes?” Wolf barked.

Wolf went to Paisley’s closet.

He wondered, “What shoes will I get?”

Wolf imagined himself in sports shoes.

WOLF
7

Wolf looked deeper into the closet.

He thought, “Maybe swimming shoes.

Nope, they would be hard to walk in.”

“Dressy shoes. That’s it,” Wolf barked.

He could see himself in tall heels.

But Paisley wobbled when she walked

in Mom’s shoes.

He decided dress shoes are not for

long walks.

Wolf said, “Yee-haw, cowboy boots would be fun.”

On the wall hung Paisley's dance shoes. Wolf imagined gliding across the stage in ballet slippers.

He remembered Mom saying that dance shoes are not for outside.

He decided he needed shoes for walking outdoors.

Wolf got an idea … combat boots.
Paisley’s mom wears combat boots
as a police officer.
He pretended to be on a chase.

PPD

“Police work is hard. I need a nap.”

Wolf found his special spot in front of the window and curled up to sleep.

Wolf dreamed of all kinds of shoes.

Wolf woke up.

Rattle, rattle...thump.
He heard a noise outside.

His tail wagged at the thought of seeing Paisley.

Mom carried a shopping bag.

The bag smelled like the pet store.

Wolf did his happy dance.

PET SHOP

Mom took shoes out of the sack. Paisley asked, “Can Wolf wear his shoes?”

“Come here boy,” Mom put the shoes on Wolf.

The shoes felt funny and made him step carefully.

"He will get used to them," Mom said.

Paisley attached Wolf’s leash.
“Let’s go for a walk”.

Wolf got used to walking in the shoes. He loved how the new shoes protected his paws from the hot sidewalk.

Can you match the shoes?

Rebecca Ballew Dockum and Wolf, her dog, explored her family's farm deep in the wooded Missouri Ozarks. She began story telling as a child. Who wouldn't develop an imagination with nearby towns named Tightwad and Toad Suck?

Today, Rebecca lives in Phoenix, Arizona where she writes children's books and practices silversmithing.

Rebecca believes ordinary people can do extraordinary things.

Tim Traylor specializes in colored pencil. During his deployment to Vietnam, he created cartoons for Stars & Stripes.

He continues his art by illustrating wildlife, western themes, and aviation.

Tim enjoys spending time with his new puppy, Jazzy.

Alysha Coy Desharnais considers herself a maker and loves exploring new projects and mediums. She has a love of textiles and fiber arts that started early in her childhood.

Alysha lives in Western Massachusetts where she fills her time with sewing, knitting, and taking long walks with her dog Kia.

Printed in the USA
CPSIA information can be obtained
at www.ICGtesting.com
CBHW042339261024
16376CB00004B/45

9 798988 133117